"The same way you influence your surroundings, your surroundings influence you". ~ Forbes Sisters

Who or what influences you? _____

_____

_____

_____

_____

_____

How are you influenced? _____

_____

_____

_____

_____

_____

_____

_____

Are these influences positive or negative? _____

_____

_____

_____

_____

_____

_____

What, if anything, do you need to change? _____

_____

_____

_____

_____

_____

_____

_____

_____

_____

"Patience is the weapon that forces

deception to reveal itself..."

~ Dr. Murdoch

What have you learned about yourself while waiting for something to occur? _____

_____

_____

_____

_____

_____

_____

_____

_____

_____

_____

_____

_____

_____

_____

Would the outcome have been different if you would have completed a task while you waited?

_____

_____

_____

_____

_____

_____

_____

_____

_____

_____

_____

_____

_____

It's funny how so much of finding yourself in adulthood is simply getting back to who you were and what you loved as a child.

What are some things you loved as a child? _____

What version of that could you incorporate into your current lifestyle? _____

_____

_____

_____

_____

_____

_____

_____

_____

_____

_____

_____

_____

_____

_____

I might have to be what I never had.

What is something that you have always needed or

wanted someone else to be to or for you? _____

_____

_____

_____

_____

_____

_____

_____

_____

_____

_____

_____

_____

_____

_____

How can you be that for yourself? _____

_____

_____

_____

_____

_____

_____

_____

_____

_____

_____

_____

_____

_____

Never regret anything because at one time it was exactly what you wanted.

What is something you wanted but now you realize it was not what was best for you? _____

_____

_____

_____

_____

_____

_____

_____

_____

_____

_____

_____

_____

_____

How have you changed since you had that desire?

_____

_____

_____

_____

_____

_____

_____

_____

_____

_____

_____

_____

_____

_____

_____

"Sometimes you're not in trouble, you're in training". – Steven Furtick

Think about a time in which you were in "trouble". How did that situation prepare you for where you are today? _____

_____

_____

_____

_____

_____

_____

_____

_____

_____

_____

_____

_____

_____

How does this training impact your actions today?

_____

_____

_____

_____

_____

_____

_____

_____

_____

_____

_____

_____

_____

_____

The greatest power we possess is

the power of choice.

What choices have you made in the past six months?

_____

_____

_____

_____

_____

_____

_____

_____

_____

_____

_____

_____

_____

_____

How have those choices impacted your life?_____

_____

_____

_____

_____

_____

_____

_____

Would you do anything different?_____

_____

_____

_____

_____

_____

_____

_____

Take note of your own faults and

leave others' alone.

Take a good look at yourself. List three faults/flaws?

_____

_____

_____

_____

_____

_____

_____

_____

_____

_____

_____

_____

_____

_____

How do you perceive others with these same faults or flaws? _____

_____

_____

_____

_____

_____

_____

_____

_____

_____

_____

_____

_____

_____

"It is in sharing your deepest truth with another that you create the space for potentially more love and freedom". ~ Kute Blackson

Who in your life have or can you share your deepest truth, without judgement? _____

_____

_____

_____

_____

_____

_____

_____

_____

_____

_____

_____

_____

_____

How would you define that relationship? _____

_____

_____

_____

_____

_____

_____

_____

_____

_____

_____

_____

_____

_____

"Courage is the human virtue that counts most. Courage to act on limited knowledge and insufficient evidence. That's all any of us have"
– Robert Frost

What is something you wish you had more courage to do? _____

_____

_____

_____

_____

_____

_____

_____

_____

_____

_____

_____

_____

_____

How would your life differ if you took a chance and did "it"? _____

_____

_____

_____

_____

_____

_____

_____

_____

_____

_____

_____

_____

_____

_____

Sometimes it's the change that I fight the most, that is the change that I need the most.

What is one change that would have the most impact on your life? _____

_____

_____

_____

_____

_____

_____

_____

_____

_____

_____

_____

_____

_____

_____

_____

What is your hesitation in making this change?

_____

_____

_____

_____

_____

_____

_____

_____

_____

_____

_____

_____

_____

_____

Sometimes that which I fear to lose is that which I would benefit from letting go.

What is something that you need to release? ___

What do you benefit from holding on to it? _____

_____

_____

_____

_____

_____

_____

_____

_____

_____

_____

_____

_____

_____

_____

_____

Responding to the past in the present can stagnate one's future.

What is something from your past that you bring into your current relationship(s)? _____

_____

_____

_____

_____

_____

_____

_____

_____

_____

_____

_____

_____

_____

How would your relationship(s) differ it you let that thing go? _____

_____

_____

_____

_____

_____

_____

_____

_____

_____

_____

_____

_____

_____

_____

"Great minds discuss ideas. Average minds discuss events. Small minds discuss people". ~ Eleanor Roosevelt

Think about your last three conversations. What were the topics of discussion? _____

_____

_____

_____

_____

_____

_____

_____

_____

_____

_____

_____

_____

_____

_____

How could your conversations improve? _____

"The fall hurt like hell, but I found grace in the wounds and a version of me I never knew". ~ Unknown

Think about your most recent "wound". What did it teach you about yourself? _____

_____

_____

_____

_____

_____

_____

_____

_____

_____

_____

_____

_____

_____

How can you use what the "wound" as fuel to reach your goals? _____

_____

_____

_____

_____

_____

_____

_____

_____

_____

_____

_____

_____

_____

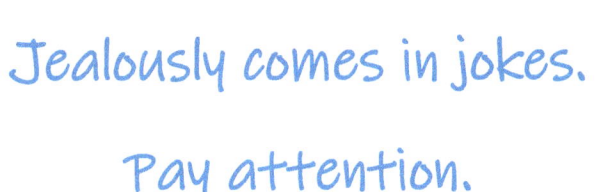

Jealously comes in jokes.

Pay attention.

Think about the last time you shared a success with someone. How did they respond? _____

_____

_____

_____

_____

_____

_____

_____

_____

_____

_____

_____

_____

_____

Think about the last time someone shared a success with you. How did you respond? _____

_____

_____

_____

_____

_____

_____

_____

_____

_____

_____

_____

_____

_____

High standards protect you from low quality experiences.

Think about the past six months. What has been the quality of your experiences? _____

_____

_____

_____

_____

_____

_____

_____

_____

_____

_____

_____

_____

_____

Think about your expectations of these experiences.

Do you need to make some adjustments? _____

_____

_____

_____

_____

_____

_____

_____

_____

_____

_____

_____

_____

_____

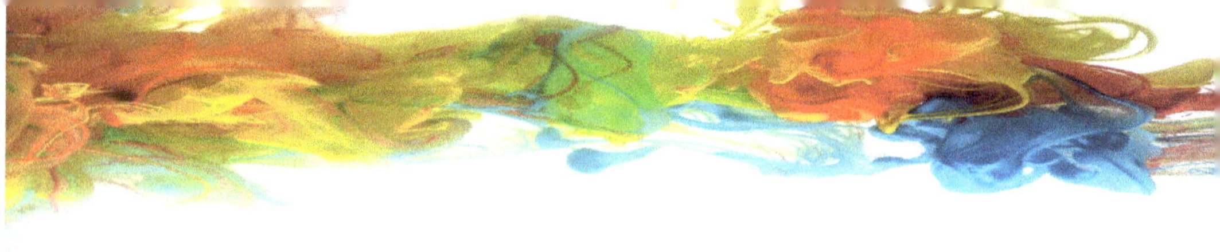

Stop falling in love with fairytales.

Work on you!

Fall in love with yourself.

What is a fairytale that you hold? _____

_____

_____

_____

_____

_____

_____

_____

_____

_____

_____

_____

_____

_____

_____

_____

How would your life differ is you loved yourself the way you are waiting on someone else to love you?

_____

_____

_____

_____

_____

_____

_____

_____

_____

_____

_____

_____

_____

You stay focused on the mountain but let's talk about your mood.

Let's be honest, some days your mood is foul. How has your mood impacted your progress? _____

_____

_____

_____

_____

_____

_____

_____

_____

_____

_____

_____

_____

_____

How would things in your life look if your mood was different? _____

_____

_____

_____

_____

_____

_____

_____

_____

_____

_____

_____

_____

_____

Are you wide in your activity but

shallow in your impact?

Are you doing things just to say you did them or are you making an impact? What proof do you have?

_____

_____

_____

_____

_____

_____

_____

_____

_____

_____

_____

_____

_____

_____

List how your past three activities impacted you and others?

_____

_____

_____

_____

_____

_____

_____

_____

_____

_____

_____

_____

_____

_____

where would you be if you had not

stopped?

Things happen, that's a part of life. What happened in your life that made you "stop"? _____

_____

_____

_____

_____

_____

_____

_____

_____

_____

_____

_____

_____

_____

_____

How would your life differ if you had kept going?

_____

_____

_____

_____

_____

_____

_____

_____

_____

_____

_____

_____

_____

_____

It's not what they said but how you processed it.

How are processing what others tell you? _____

How would things improve if you processed the information differently? _____

_____

_____

_____

_____

_____

_____

_____

_____

_____

_____

_____

_____

_____

Sometimes we are destroyed by something that isn't destructive.

When is the last time something good caused you harm?
_____

_____

_____

_____

_____

_____

_____

_____

_____

_____

_____

_____

_____

_____

Was this harm caused by your own thought(s) or the action of another? _____

_____

_____

_____

_____

_____

_____

_____

_____

_____

_____

_____

_____

_____

"Miserable people focus on what they hate about their life. Happy people focus on what they love about their life". – Zig Ziglar

Where is your current focus? _____

_____

_____

_____

_____

_____

_____

_____

_____

_____

_____

_____

_____

_____

_____

_____

Do you seem to be more problem or solution focused? _____

_____

_____

_____

_____

_____

_____

_____

_____

_____

_____

_____

_____

_____

Your mood will impact your movement.

Describe your current mood. _____

_____

_____

_____

_____

_____

_____

_____

_____

_____

_____

_____

_____

_____

_____

_____

_____

What impact has your mood had on your day? _

_____

_____

_____

_____

_____

_____

_____

_____

_____

_____

_____

_____

_____

_____

A mistake that makes you humble is better than an achievement that makes you arrogant.

What is the best lesson you have learned thus far?

_____

_____

_____

_____

_____

_____

_____

_____

_____

_____

_____

_____

_____

_____

_____

_____

Did this lesson humble or change you? If so, how?

_____

_____

_____

_____

_____

_____

_____

_____

_____

_____

_____

_____

_____

_____

Go be your favorite self.
We are used to hearing, "be your best" but being your favorite, allows room for grace.

What would your life look like if you lived it based

on your favorite self? _____

_____

_____

_____

_____

_____

_____

_____

_____

_____

_____

_____

_____

_____

_____

What keeps you from being your favorite version of you? _____

_____

_____

_____

_____

_____

_____

_____

_____

_____

_____

_____

_____

_____

You're going to piss off a lot of people when you start doing what is best for you. Do it anyway!

What are five things you need to do, specifically for your own benefit? _____

_____

_____

_____

_____

_____

_____

_____

_____

_____

_____

_____

_____

_____

_____

Who in your life will not be pleased about these changes? Why? _____

_____

_____

_____

_____

_____

_____

_____

_____

_____

_____

_____

_____

_____

"You can't look around at everyone else, expecting to have joy. You can't judge your situation according to other people's calling and expect to have joy. You can't measure your gift compared to other people's talent and expect joy. Nothing destroys joy like comparison". ~ Unknown

How does comparison to others impact your joy?

_____

_____

_____

_____

_____

_____

_____

_____

_____

_____

_____

_____

_____

_____

_____

_____

How would your life be impacted if you focused on yourself? _____

_____

_____

_____

_____

_____

_____

_____

_____

_____

_____

_____

_____

_____

_____

"We can't solve our problems with the same level of consciousness that created them". ~ Albert Einstein

Think about your thought process during a negative situation. How does your thinking impact your ability to develop a solution? _____

_____

_____

_____

_____

_____

_____

_____

_____

_____

_____

_____

_____

_____

_____

How can being more solution focused impact your wellbeing? _____

_____

_____

_____

_____

_____

_____

_____

_____

_____

_____

_____

_____

_____

_____

_____

"When things change in you, things around you change". ~ Olivia Rink

What are some internal changes you can make within the next 30 days? _____

_____

_____

_____

_____

_____

_____

_____

_____

_____

_____

_____

_____

_____

_____

How will these changes impact you externally? _

_____

_____

_____

_____

_____

_____

_____

_____

_____

_____

_____

_____

_____

_____

You have enough time; your priorities

are just messed up.

List three things you would like to do but feel you don't have the time? _____

_____

_____

_____

_____

_____

_____

_____

_____

_____

_____

_____

_____

_____

How would changing your priorities impact your ability to accomplish these things?_____

_____

_____

_____

_____

_____

_____

_____

_____

_____

_____

_____

_____

_____

If someone wanted to, they would.

Think about where you spend most of your time. Is this where you want to be? _____

_____

_____

_____

_____

_____

_____

_____

_____

_____

_____

_____

_____

_____

What keeps you from making the time? _____

_____

_____

_____

_____

_____

_____

_____

_____

_____

_____

_____

_____

_____

Loyalty is often conditional.

Describe what loyalty means to you. _____

_____

_____

_____

_____

_____

_____

_____

_____

_____

_____

_____

_____

_____

_____

_____

Does your loyalty come with conditions? If so, why?

_____

_____

_____

_____

_____

_____

_____

_____

_____

_____

_____

_____

_____

_____

_____

"If you crave happiness enough, you will stop at nothing to get it".

~ Unknown

What do you crave? _____

_____

_____

_____

_____

_____

_____

Is your craving healthy for you? Why or why not?

_____

_____

_____

_____

_____

_____

_____

What is stopping you from getting what you want?

_____

_____

_____

_____

_____

_____

_____

_____

_____

_____

_____

_____

_____

_____

_____

"Just because you are right, does not mean I am wrong. You just haven't seen life from my side."

~ Daily Thoughts

Write about one thing that occurred in your life that most people don't know about you._____

_____

_____

_____

_____

_____

_____

_____

_____

_____

_____

_____

_____

_____

How does this "thing" impact your relationships?

_____

_____

_____

_____

_____

_____

_____

_____

_____

_____

_____

_____

_____

_____

We pick our friends, but real

situations sort them out.

What is one situation in your life that revealed your true friends? _____

_____

_____

_____

_____

_____

_____

_____

_____

_____

_____

_____

_____

_____

What is one situation in your life that exposed who wasn't as real as you originally thought? _____

_____

_____

_____

_____

_____

_____

_____

_____

_____

_____

_____

_____

_____

I am often the headache and the
medicine.

When is the last time in your life that you were the problem and the solution? _____

_____

_____

_____

_____

_____

_____

_____

_____

_____

_____

_____

_____

_____

_____

Is it easier for you to identify as the problem or the solution? _____

_____
_____
_____
_____
_____
_____
_____
_____
_____
_____
_____
_____
_____
_____

People who wait to see you win will
be willing to help you win.

Think about the people in your life. Who is always there cheering you on, showing support, offering help? _____

_____

_____

_____

_____

_____

_____

_____

_____

_____

_____

_____

_____

_____

Think about the people in your life. Who seems to cheer but doesn't celebrate the wins or offer help?

_____

_____

_____

_____

_____

_____

_____

_____

_____

_____

_____

_____

_____

"One of the greatest hazards in life

is to risk nothing". ~ Leo Buscaglia

When is the last time you took a risk? _____

_____

_____

_____

_____

_____

_____

_____

_____

_____

_____

_____

_____

_____

_____

What was the reward and/or lesson? _____

_____

_____

_____

_____

_____

_____

_____

_____

_____

_____

_____

_____

_____

_____

_____

_____

Be kind, be respectful, but take no shit.

Where in your life do you need to set boundaries?

_____

_____

_____

_____

_____

_____

_____

_____

_____

_____

_____

_____

_____

_____

_____

_____

How will these boundaries impact your growth?

_____

_____

_____

_____

_____

_____

_____

_____

_____

_____

_____

_____

_____

_____

_____

_____

"Do things from love not for love".

~ Unknown

When is the last time you did something for someone that could not do anything for you? ___

_____

_____

_____

_____

_____

_____

_____

_____

_____

_____

_____

_____

_____

How do you respond when people do for you with no expectation that you will reciprocate? _____

_____

_____

_____

_____

_____

_____

_____

_____

_____

_____

_____

_____

_____

Failure is a part of life.

Think about the last time you failed. What did you learn about yourself? _____

_____

_____

_____

_____

_____

_____

_____

_____

_____

_____

_____

_____

_____

What did you learn about those around you? ___

Everyone has an addiction to something.

Legal or illegal, what's your vice? _____

How do you treat others that have vices/addictions different from yours? _____

_____

_____

_____

_____

_____

_____

_____

_____

_____

_____

_____

_____

_____

Imagine going through an entire day being unapologetically you.

How would your day go from start to finish if you spent an entire day being your authentic self? __

_____

_____

_____

_____

_____

_____

_____

_____

_____

_____

_____

_____

_____

How would those around you respond to you being your authentic self? _____

_____

_____

_____

_____

_____

_____

_____

_____

_____

_____

_____

_____

_____

_____

Sometimes you must fall back and let them rely on those they think so highly of.

Think about the people in your life. Do you need to distance yourself from any of them? _____

_____

_____

_____

_____

_____

_____

_____

_____

_____

_____

_____

_____

_____

Why have you held onto these relationships? ___

_____

_____

_____

_____

_____

_____

_____

_____

_____

_____

_____

_____

_____

_____

Let it hurt.

Forgive.

Let it heal.

Think about your past. What is something that
resulted in you feeling hurt? _____

_____

_____

_____

_____

_____

_____

_____

_____

_____

_____

_____

_____

_____

_____

Write an apology/forgiveness note to yourself.__

_____

_____

_____

_____

_____

_____

_____

_____

_____

_____

_____

_____

_____

_____

_____

_____

_____

Today I forgive myself for all the mistakes I made simply because I was tired or emotionally overwhelmed.

Assess how you've felt over the past six months.

Have you been tired, overwhelmed, anxious? ___

_____

_____

_____

_____

_____

_____

_____

_____

_____

_____

_____

_____

_____

_____

What can you do this week to engage in self-care?

_____

_____

_____

_____

_____

_____

_____

_____

_____

_____

_____

_____

_____

_____

_____

I'll give you the benefit of doubt

until I can't.

Think about the people in your life. Who have you given the benefit of doubt more times than you should have? _____

_____

_____

_____

_____

_____

_____

_____

_____

_____

_____

_____

_____

_____

Why do you keep this person in your life? What's the benefit? _____

_____

_____

_____

_____

_____

_____

_____

_____

_____

_____

_____

_____

_____

_____

_____

People despise what they don't

understand.

Who do you distance yourself from because you don't understand them or their situation? _____

_____

_____

_____

_____

_____

_____

_____

_____

_____

_____

_____

_____

_____

Have you had relationships end because the other person did not understand you or something about you? _____

_____

_____

_____

_____

_____

_____

_____

_____

_____

_____

_____

_____

_____

_____

_____

When you find fault with everyone
around you don't forget that you are
the common denominator.

When is the last time you took a good look in the mirror to examine you and the way you go about things? _____

_____

_____

_____

_____

_____

_____

_____

_____

_____

_____

_____

_____

_____

Take 2 minutes. Look into a mirror. Look beyond what you see on the surface. What do you see?

_____

_____

_____

_____

_____

_____

_____

_____

_____

_____

_____

_____

_____

_____

If you don't know where or how I got my scars, watch how you talk about others around me.

How do you handle situations in which others speak negatively about someone that is going through something that is a part of your past? _____

_____

_____

_____

_____

_____

_____

_____

_____

_____

_____

_____

_____

_____

How can you offer support to the person that is in the situation?

_____

_____

_____

_____

_____

_____

_____

_____

_____

_____

_____

_____

_____

_____

Not one of my friends have ever came back and told me what someone else has said about me.

How do you discern who is a true friend and who is taking up space in your life? _____

_____

_____

_____

_____

_____

_____

_____

_____

_____

_____

_____

_____

_____

What steps can you take to ensure you spend more time with the people who support and challenge you to be a better person? _____

_____

_____

_____

_____

_____

_____

_____

_____

_____

_____

_____

_____

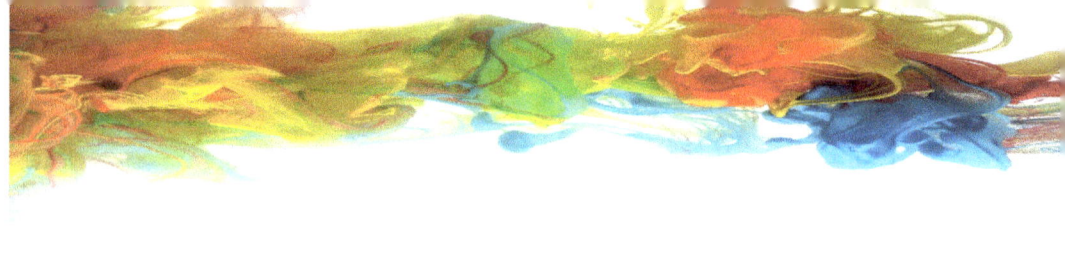

The problem with putting others first is you've taught yourself to be okay with second.

What can you start doing to put yourself in the position of first? _____

_____

_____

_____

_____

_____

_____

_____

_____

_____

_____

_____

_____

_____

_____

_____

How will making you a priority impact those in your life? _____

_____

_____

_____

_____

_____

_____

_____

_____

_____

_____

_____

_____

_____

Just because the love is real doesn't
mean the information is right.

List 5 things and 5 people that you love but aren't right for what you are currently doing with your life.

_____

_____

_____

_____

_____

_____

_____

_____

_____

_____

_____

_____

_____

_____

_____

_____

List reasons why these people or things shouldn't continue the journey with you. _____

_____

_____

_____

_____

_____

_____

_____

_____

_____

_____

_____

_____

_____

"The thing that makes you exceptional, if you are at all, is inevitably that which makes you lonely". ~ Lorraine Hansberry

List three (3) things that make you exceptional and why. _____

_____

_____

_____

_____

_____

_____

_____

_____

_____

_____

_____

_____

_____

How do or could these three things contribute to you feeling lonely? _____

_____

_____

_____

_____

_____

_____

_____

_____

_____

_____

_____

_____

_____

_____

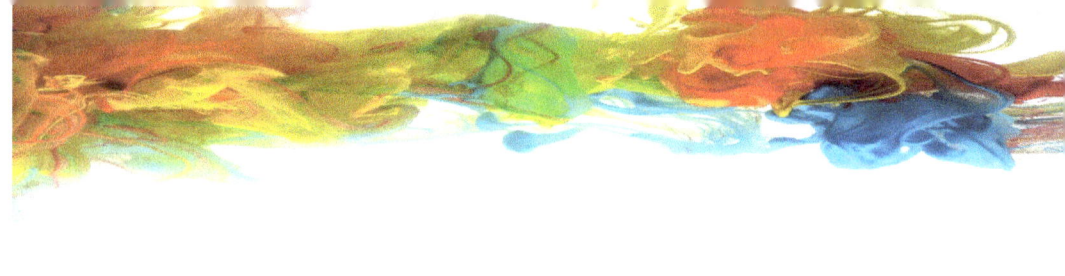

"The mess occurs in the middle".

~ Dr. Darius Daniels

Think about your life. What areas contain mess?

_____

_____

_____

_____

_____

_____

_____

_____

_____

_____

_____

_____

_____

_____

_____

What are some things you can do to eliminate the mess? _____

_____

_____

_____

_____

_____

_____

_____

_____

_____

_____

_____

_____

You could live a better life if you mind your own business.

How often do you find yourself monitoring others via social media or gossip? What do you get out of minding the business of others? _____

_____

_____

_____

_____

_____

_____

_____

_____

_____

_____

_____

_____

_____

How would your life differ if you spent that time assessing your own life? _____

_____

_____

_____

_____

_____

_____

_____

_____

_____

_____

_____

_____

_____

You either quit or keep going.

They both hurt.

What keeps you moving toward your goals? ____

_____

_____

_____

_____

_____

_____

_____

_____

_____

_____

_____

_____

_____

_____

What slows you down and interferes with your progress?_____

_____

_____

_____

_____

_____

_____

_____

_____

_____

_____

_____

_____

_____

Pay attention to when and why

people want to talk to you.

Think about your relationships. Who do you talk to the most? _____

_____

_____

_____

_____

What do you get out of those conversations?____

_____

_____

_____

_____

_____

_____

_____

Who in your life seeks you out to talk? _____

_____

_____

_____

_____

_____

_____

How do they benefit from those conversations?_

_____

_____

_____

_____

_____

_____

_____

Stress, anxiety, and depression are often caused when we are living to please others.

How often do you feel stress, anxiety and/or

depression? _____

_____

_____

_____

_____

_____

_____

_____

_____

_____

_____

_____

_____

_____

How often do you find yourself attempting to please others?_____

_____

_____

_____

_____

How would your level of stress, anxiety, or depression change, if you spent more time doing what you need to do for you?_____

_____

_____

_____

_____

_____

_____

_____

Don't let people you love sabotage your success. The truth is, if they love you, they'll want you to be successful. Sabotage is jealousy and control.

Love is setting you up for success.

Who in your life "sets you up for success"? _____

_____

_____

_____

_____

_____

How do you know this is what they are doing? __

_____

_____

_____

_____

_____

_____

_____

Who in your life appears jealous and/or attempts to control your decisions? _____

_____

_____

_____

_____

_____

Why are they in your life?_____

_____

_____

_____

_____

_____

_____

_____

"A jealous demon will try to disguise itself as a supportive angel, be watchful". ~ Unknown

Think about your relationships. Identify two people that support your growth. _____

_____

_____

_____

_____

How are they supportive? _____

_____

_____

_____

_____

_____

_____

_____

_____

Identify two people in your life that appear supportive but are not?_____

_____

_____

_____

_____

Why do you maintain these relationships?_____

_____

_____

_____

_____

_____

_____

_____

_____

_____

The real flex is healing yourself
without becoming like those who
traumatized you.

Think about the past six months. What things have you done to work towards healing yourself? ___

_____

_____

_____

_____

_____

_____

_____

_____

_____

_____

_____

_____

_____

What are healthy things you can do during the next six months to continue this process? _____

_____

_____

_____

_____

_____

_____

_____

_____

_____

_____

_____

_____

Forget the mistake, remember the lesson.

Think about the last mistake you made. How did it impact you?_____

_____

_____

_____

_____

_____

_____

_____

_____

_____

_____

_____

_____

What did you learn about yourself because of this mistake? _____

_____

_____

_____

_____

_____

_____

_____

_____

_____

_____

_____

_____

Sometimes the pit is God's favor.

Think about the past 10 years. List three moments in which you felt as if you were at your lowest, in the pit. _____

_____

_____

_____

_____

_____

_____

_____

_____

_____

_____

_____

_____

Thinking about those moments, how do you now see God's favor? _____

_____

_____

_____

_____

_____

_____

_____

_____

_____

_____

_____

_____

"Love is an action, never simply a feeling". ~ bell hooks

Think about your relationships. What are things someone can do to show you love? _____

_____

_____

_____

_____

_____

_____

_____

_____

_____

_____

_____

_____

_____

_____

_____

What are things that you do to show others love?

_____

_____

_____

_____

_____

_____

Do you show love based on who you would like to

receive it from others?_____

_____

_____

_____

_____

_____

_____

"There are blessings on the back roads". ~ Steven Furtick

Back roads tend to have fewer stops but are more challenging to navigate. Think about challenges you've experienced over the past two weeks. Identify how you felt in those moments? _____

_____

_____

_____

_____

_____

_____

_____

_____

_____

_____

_____

Identify how those challenges are or may have been blessings? _____

_____

_____

_____

_____

_____

_____

_____

_____

_____

_____

_____

_____

_____

Letting shit slide to keep the peace

will start a war on the inside of you.

Think about the people in your life. Who do you need to start holding accountable for their actions?

_____

_____

_____

_____

_____

_____

_____

_____

_____

_____

_____

_____

_____

_____

Do you think you will have more peace or war when you hold them accountable? Why?_____

_____

_____

_____

_____

_____

_____

_____

_____

_____

_____

_____

_____

_____

"When you entertain a clown, you become a part of the circus".

~ Unknown

Think about the past week. What have been some things that you have entertained but should not?

_____

_____

_____

_____

_____

_____

_____

_____

_____

_____

_____

_____

_____

What are things you can do differently so that you don't become a part of the "circus"? _____

_____

_____

_____

_____

_____

_____

_____

_____

_____

_____

_____

_____

_____

"Sometimes it takes losing what you settled for to remind you of what you truly deserve". ~ Rania Naim

Think about the past year. What are some areas of your life in which you have settled for less? _____

_____

_____

_____

_____

_____

_____

_____

_____

_____

_____

_____

_____

_____

_____

List at least five things you deserve. _____

_____

_____

_____

_____

_____

_____

_____

_____

_____

_____

_____

_____

_____

_____

_____

You can love them, but you can't heal them. That's their journey, not yours.

Who are you trying to heal? _____

_____

_____

_____

_____

_____

_____

_____

_____

_____

_____

_____

_____

_____

What would happen in your life if you put that same energy into healing and loving yourself? _____

_____

_____

_____

_____

_____

_____

_____

_____

_____

_____

_____

_____

_____

"You don't need to be seen to know the power you hold". ~ Taraney Nicole

What power to you hold down on the inside? ___

_____

_____

_____

_____

_____

_____

_____

_____

_____

_____

_____

_____

_____

How would your relationships with others change if you allowed that power to surface? _____

_____

_____

_____

_____

_____

_____

_____

_____

_____

_____

_____

_____

_____

The truth doesn't mind being

questioned but a lie does.

Often the truth scares us, so we wear a mask to camouflage what's real. What aspects of your life do you struggle with being questioned? _____

_____

_____

_____

_____

_____

_____

_____

_____

_____

_____

_____

_____

How would your life differ if you lived out your truth, instead of putting on a mask? _____

_____

_____

_____

_____

_____

_____

_____

_____

_____

_____

_____

_____

_____

You cannot love and judge at the
same time.

How often are you judgmental towards yourself?

_____

_____

_____

_____

_____

How do you benefit?_____

_____

_____

_____

_____

_____

_____

_____

How does this make you feel about you? _____

_____

_____

_____

_____

_____

_____

_____

_____

_____

_____

_____

_____

_____

_____

Some people will never ask for your side of the story because the side they heard fits the description of how they want to feel about you.

What is the last thing you "heard" about yourself?

_____

_____

_____

_____

_____

_____

_____

_____

_____

_____

_____

_____

_____

Was this information based on fact or someone's perception of you? _____

_____

_____

_____

_____

_____

_____

Did this impact how you felt about yourself? _____

_____

_____

_____

_____

_____

_____

_____

Sometimes you need a "stop doing" list just as bad as you need a "to-do" list.

Write out your "Stop Doing" list for the next six months.

_____

_____

_____

_____

_____

_____

_____

_____

_____

_____

_____

_____

_____

_____

How will this list impact your "To-Do" list for the next six months? _____

_____

_____

_____

_____

_____

_____

_____

_____

_____

_____

_____

_____

_____

_____

Thank you for taking the time to work on you.

As we learn and grow, we realize that the things we have seen, done, and experienced over the years may have been normal to us; however, it doesn't necessarily mean they are right for us.

I challenge you to assess your ways of thinking.

I challenge you to become your true, authentic, favorite self.

May God continue to watch over and bless you as you continue your journey here on earth.

~ LaToya